they rule the world

they
rule
the
world

Samuel Hazo

Syracuse University Press

∞ The paper used in this publication meets the minimum requirements
of the American National Standard for Information Sciences—Permanence
of Paper for Printed Library Materials, ANSI Z39.48-1992.

For a listing of books published and distributed by Syracuse University Press,
visit www.SyracuseUniversityPress.syr.edu.

ISBN: 978-0-8156-3492-8 (hardcover)
978-0-8156-1080-9 (paperback)
978-0-8156-5390-5 (e-book)

Library of Congress Cataloging-in-Publication Data
Names: Hazo, Samuel, 1928–
Title: They rule the world / Samuel Hazo.
Description: First Edition. | Syracuse, New York : Syracuse University Press, 2016.
Identifiers: LCCN 2016018336 (print) | LCCN 2016023725 (ebook) |
ISBN 9780815634928 (hardcover : alk. paper) | ISBN 9780815610809
(pbk. : alk. paper) | ISBN 9780815653905 (ebook) | ISBN 9780815653905 (e-book)
Classification: LCC PS3515.A9877 A6 2016 (print) | LCC PS3515.A9877 (ebook) |
DDC 811/.54—dc23
LC record available at https://lccn.loc.gov/2016018336

For Mary Anne, again and always.

Contents

they rule the world

Alone with Presences

Paying my tax bill can wait.
Some huckster hawking condos
   in Belize can leave a message.
King Death can keep his terrors
   to himself for once.
                        I live
   by preference in space where clocks
   have no hands, and time
   is what it is when there is
   nothing else to think about.
Infinity takes over long enough
   for me to reunite with those
   I loved the most.
                        It eases me
   to feel they're near, which proves
   those gone are never gone.
I play backgammon with my father
   in a dream and lose and lose.
I'm talking Plato with my brother
   in Annapolis.
                        It's then and now
   where FDR and JFK stay
   quotably alive while Marilyn
   Monroe survives and thrives
   in all her blonde availability.
Are these as everlasting
   as my aunt's devotion or my mother's
   smile when she sang or how
   my brother faced his last
   Epiphany without a whimper?

Who says that those who've gone
   are ever out of sight or mind?
They're present but invisible.

                    They visit
  when they choose.
            They rule the world.

PART ONE

Born in Hiding

A Poem's Only Deadline Is Perfection

After you start to write it,
  you belong to the poem.
                            Your time
  becomes the poem's time,
  which ranges anywhere
  from now to who knows when.
You're like a sculptor working
  with mallet, wedge and file
  to help the sculpture waiting
  in a bulk of rock emerge.
Like something born in hiding,
  a poem lets itself be found
  the more you fret and work
  to free it of its flaws.
Even when the poem seems complete,
  you're still not sure of a verb here,
  an adjective there.
                    You squander
  hours searching for alternatives
  until they both occur to you
  by chance while you're thinking
  of something else entirely.
There's no timetable.
                  You pause
  when the poem makes you pause.
You write when the poem makes
  you write.
              Precedent means nothing.
Even when you think it's done,
  it's never done.

You tell yourself
you could have made it better,
but the time for bettering is over.
Being a poet means
you have to live with that.

Forever Amber

I said the light was yellow.
"Amber," stressed the Law,
   "and amber means to proceed
   with caution."
                  Already wrong
  on color and fearing further
  error, I kept still.
              "This is
  a warning," he said, "because
  you ran an amber light."
The incident reminded me
  how red, green and yellow—
  or rather amber—say it all.
With green and red I have
  no argument.
             The only options
  are compliance or defiance.
To stop on green or go
  defiantly on red would make
  for total chaos.
              Yellow—
  amber, I mean—allows
  a chooser time to think.
It's like this moment in this very
  poem when I feel I've said
  enough.
           Ambering without
  a cop in sight, I weigh
  the choice of going on or not.

For Bill Merwin Nearing Ninety

"To write a good poem," you told
  me once, "is its own award."
Later you spurned a Pulitzer
  to call attention to America's
  "civilizing mission" to Vietnamize
  the Vietnamese (in Vietnam!).
Auden, ostensibly a friend,
  accused you of publicity-seeking.
For Auden and neo-Audens,
  resistance was out of step.
While some amnesiacs who disagreed
  or were discreetly mute
  survived in their irrelevance,
  you stayed the same.
                I'm thinking
of you now in Maui, tending
your conservancy with failing
sight while managing to finish
book after book.
              Some say
that talent weakens with the years.
Your books prove age means nothing
  to poets.
            Whatever must be seen
and said you still can see
and say.
          The poems keep coming.

Linda Pastan's Fourteenth Book

You've done it again but always
  with restraint.
               You used just twenty
  words to say how seeing Ira
  for the first time changed you.
The full, fast days of a good
  marriage came of it.
               Is making
  poems any different?
               You coax
  an impulse, word by word,
  into its final self.
               Because
  you have no choice, it has
  its way with you.
               It lives
  to last with no finale.
               Conjugal
  as love at first sight,
  it keeps you wedded to your words.
Each time you say it to yourself,
  it's new as now.
               Even when
  you think it's not, it is.

Overheard

All those who listen with their eyes
   agree that silence is speech
   at its truest.
                  It's not the silence
of libraries, study halls, infirmaries,
basilicas or anywhere made quiet
by tradition, purpose or demand.
It's more than absence of sound.
Even the deaf can hear it.
Decades ago I wrote a book
   entitled *Silence Spoken Here*
   to show that silence alone
   is understandable without translation
   everywhere by everybody always.
Why else do authors in France
   gather every year in Nice
   to discuss the mystery of *Le Silence*?
I'd like to be there once
   to add my two-cents' worth
   of relevance.
                Who hasn't heard
the mute silence following
a funeral, the silent gratitude
of being remembered by coincidence
or the paired silence shared
by twins.
           Lovers after all
say everything there is to say
by saying nothing when they touch.

That's how whatever's touched
   by love reflects and then outlives
   the silence that created it.
Between the lines of poems
   hides another poem,
   everlasting but invisible.
It's what you keep on hearing
   when the poem's over . . .
                    Listen.

Solo

Now of a certain age,
  I have far fewer friends,
  but the few are truer.
All that I know seems dated,
  myself included.
                    Prospects
  of immortality no longer
  lure me nor do those honors
  seemingly awarded more
  for notoriety than worth.
                    I call
  the current primacy of film
  over books a vote for recognition
  over understanding.
                    I hear
  no poetry in oratory.
                    For me
  the trend of certain males
  to stay unbarbered and unshaven
  leaves hidden their naked faces.
Though some extol tattoos
  as body art, I see no more
  than ink injected for exhibit—
  skin-shows.
                    When mocked, I feel
  no need for self-defense unless
  provoked.
                    Before death corners me,
  I say my only options are
  to keep on doing what I do

as long as possible and leave
at least and last a good name.

PART TWO

Coping with the Obvious

Something Wrong?

"What's wrong?" was how she started
   every conversation.
                For her
the basic certainty was trouble,
   not happiness or even pleasantry.
If you assured her you were fine,
   she'd ask again, "What's wrong?"
Convinced that you were hiding
   something, she would smirk.
Ignoring honesty, she trusted
   only her suspicions . . .
                Geza
would have been her perfect foil.
A born pessimist, he sensed
   at sight how curiosity differed
   from concern.
            If asked, "What's wrong?"
he would have answered, "How
   much time do you have?"
All those familiar with his wit
   would know the question was rhetorical.
Since she was "literally correct,"
   she would have stopped to hear
   a detailed list of Geza's
   cooked-up miseries and pains.
As one who savored troubles
   a la carte, she would have relished
   every word.
            But Geza, having
trumped her nosiness with guile,

would wait until she left
to mock her in Hungarian, then laugh
the laugh that Magyars laugh
when those they mock deserve it.

Overnight

Not having seen her for more
    than a year, I expected an older
    version of a teenage girl.
Instead I saw a poised
    young woman.
                To say I was
astounded would be true, but
astounded and beguiled would be
truer.
            As one who's said
whatever ripens when ready
is where life waits, I felt
assured.
            It made me think
in similes.
                Did all the awkward
years deserve to be remembered
only as rehearsals for an unforeseen
result consummately revealed?
I asked Alice, who had
    a teenage daughter herself,
    how she reacted to the passage
    of an adolescent girl to womanhood.
She listened as a woman listens
    to the male of the species frazzled
    and befuddled while coping
    with the obvious.
                Tolerant but
not amazed, she said, "It happens."

Just Like That

Waiting, I browsed the aisle
    and gawked.
                A display of braces,
canes and crutches hung
from wall hooks.
                        Shelved
beneath them were boxes of raised
toilet seats and sanitary briefs
for women and men.
                        Fish-oil
capsules, melatonin and Biofreeze
offered total health or relief
while U-shaped pillows promised
perfect sleep.
                    After I paid
my bill, I glimpsed a stripe
of printing pasted on the counter:
"Practice random kindness
and senseless acts of beauty."
That changed a store devoted
    to the prose of remedies for pain
    into the laissez-faire of poetry.
                                Why
was I shocked?
                    I'd known
for years that anything poetic
happens by surprise, enlightening
as much as lightening, wherever
and whenever.
                    Just weeks ago

little Sarah exclaimed, "Today
is Friday, but sometimes it's Tuesday."
Equally original was what
she said this morning when she woke,
"It's pitch light outside."
And there was that total stranger
who saw me frowning between
flights and said, "Smile,
you're in Pittsburgh."
                          And so
I smiled.
                          And everyone who overheard
him smiled in the selfsame way
that you are smiling now.

Afterlives

Because the smell of leather
  being cured offended her,
  Catherine de Medici prodded
  the glove-makers in Provence to seek
  a less malodorous occupation.
She knew that jasmine grew wild
  on the Riviera and that the ichor
  of jasmine was the essence of scent.
Blended with compatible aromas,
  the mix resulted in perfume.
Glove-makers became thereafter
  glove-perfumers, then simply
  perfumers when the glovers
  moved north.
               In France today
  the leading export is perfume.
That's all because of Catherine
  de Medici.
               Acknowledged or not,
  the names of women rise
  beyond dismissal when paired
  with what endures: Cleopatra,
  Joan of Arc and one shah's
  third wife enshrined forever
  in the Taj Mahal.
               Surviving
  as memorials or myths at times
  surprises and confuses.
               Sub-zero
  islands in the Arctic and the total

frozen surface of Antarctica
commemorate Elizabeth and Maud,
both queens.
     Why them?
       Why there?

"Attention, Attention Must Finally Be Paid to Such a Person"

The title sounded like a tired
    headline without resonance—
Death of a Salesman.
                    Nothing
    could stop me from going.
                        After
    walking twenty-seven blocks
    to the Morasco, I paid three dollars
    for a seat in the fourth row center.
Behind me sat Charlie Spivak,
    whose trumpeting I knew.
                        Seconds
    before the lights dimmed,
    a tall man took an aisle seat
    in my very row.
                    It was
Arthur Miller come to watch
Lee J. Cobb, Mildred Dunnock,
Arthur Kennedy, Cameron
Mitchell and (possibly) Dustin
Hoffman as young Bernard
create his play.
                    By the time
    it ended, I was changed.
                        Leaving,
I passed John Garfield
    in the lobby.
                    He seemed as moved
    as I was, but even more so.

Re-walking twenty-seven blocks
    to my hotel, I felt historical.
Later I would boast I'd seen
    the original (for me the only)
    cast.
                Once on a writers'
    panel chaired by Arthur Miller,
    I asked if Hoffman was
    the *first* Bernard.
                        He nodded.
But that seemed trivial
    beside the memory of such
    a play consummately designed
    (Mielziner), directed (Kazan)
    and staged.
                Over the years
    I witnessed Thomas Mitchell,
    Frederic March, an older
    Hoffman and Brian Dennehy
    as Willie Loman, but none
    could rival Cobb and *the* cast.
Back at the hotel my father
    asked me the name of the play.
A salesman himself, he looked
    both disappointed and offended
    when he heard the humdrum title
    and wondered why I went.

Yes

Nora Barnacle preferred
  James Joyce the tenor
  to Joyce the writer.
                   She
  compared him to McCormick
  but thought his writings trivial.
Even after *Dubliners*
  appeared, they lived like paupers
  in Zurich, Trieste and Paris.
One critic said, "In *Dubliners*
  Joyce never wrote better—
  just differently later."
               If *later*
  meant *Ulysses*, he had
  a point.
         "You have to be
  from Dublin to understand *Ulysses*,"
  declared one Irishman.
He had a point as well.
After the publishing struggles,
  the smuggling of copies from Paris,
  the legal hassles and the pirated
  editions, *Ulysses* found
  its place.
         Judged legally
  literary were nipples, scrotums,
  sphincters and the grunts, squeals
  and utterings of lovers coupling
  in the very act.
         One wife's

unpunctuated ramble sold
more books than all the praise
combined of Eliot, Pound,
Fitzgerald, Faulkner, Hemingway
and even Einstein.
                    Molly Bloom's
soliloquy attracted millions
and attracts them still.
                    Derived
from letters to an Irish tenor
from his wife, Molly's monologue
in fact explains just how
Ulysses happened and ended.
Joyce must have known
    that Nora Barnacle, who loved
    his voice but not his books,
    would have the final word.

Remember Robinson Jeffers

He hauled from shore each stone
   by hand to build it facing
   the Pacific.
               Boulders and rounded
rocks became a tower
Yeats himself would certainly
   have called authentic.
             It's open
now to visitors as Hawk Tower
next to Tor House in Carmel
near bungalows and putting greens.
And it's preserved intact.
Scolding the perishing republic
   and writing poetry by candlelight
   became his life.
           In photographs
he looks incapable of humor,
and his eyes are the eyes
of a marksman, aiming.
            Una
and their twin sons surely
must have seen another side
of him, but that's as unapparent
as his Pittsburgh roots.
           It was
for Una that he built the tower,
mortaring and hefting every day
for forty-seven months.
           She died
twelve years ahead of him.

At seventy-five he jotted down
  six words that said what mattered
  more to him than all his poetry,
  "I shall be with you shortly."

PART THREE

Catching Up

Father and Son

1

I must be shrinking.
                    He seems
  much taller than he was
  a year ago.
                    And wiser.
He has his mother's kindness
  and the gift of spotting fakery
  at sight.
                    He works at what
he loves where clocks have no
credentials.
                    His music lasts
like love, and those who play it
tell him that.
                    Though
family means most, completing
what needs doing ranks first
with him.
                    That's why I love him
as the son-husband-father
who's exceeded every hope
I dared to have.
                    He's all
I wanted most but more
than I deserve.
                    Though two,
we're one enough to know what's
dearer than love of friend

for friend or brother for brother.
That's ours now and always.

2

We pitched and caught with mitts
   we never could dispose of—
   their weathered leather supple
   after thirty years, their pockets
   shaped by pitches gloved
   as strikes, their webbings frayed,
   their colors curing into faded
   tans obscured with dirt
   that scuffed their trademarks
   to a smudge but still left readable
   the names of Campanella and the great
   DiMaggio before each man
   was chosen for the Hall of Fame,
   then claimed in turn by paraplegia
   and infarction after Brooklyn opted
   for Los Angeles while Stengel's Yankees
   kept their pinstripes in the Bronx,
   and we survived to treasure
   two outdated mitts now good
   for nothing but nostalgia every time
   we flex our fingers in them
   to be sure the past still fits.

Nothing Else or More to Say

Sometimes I resemble a retired
    actor speaking lines that worked
    well once and might work well
    again.
                One remedy might be
    to act like Maura in her nineties,
    hearing and observing in a halo
    of silence but saying not a word
    unless necessity demanded it.
Of course, there is a counter-
    argument.
                        If what was spoken
    first was perfect once,
    why not repeat it just to prove
    perfection is beyond improvement?
Tell me a better compliment
    than saying to an honest foe,
    "Here's wishing you a reasonable
    amount of luck."
                            Or mentioning
    to those who judge you by your age,
    "I won't disappoint you by not
    dying."
                Or telling anyone
    who seeks real happiness alone,
    "If love's the final happiness,
    it seems to come in pairs."
It could be age or laziness
    that makes me say these words

again, but then it could be
something else entirely.

In the Beginning

Since life is breath, and breath
  makes words, and words say what
  we mean, I offer these conclusions.
Gossip?
           Lethal and vain
  as bullets.
                 Humor?
                          Purest
  among clowns and children.
Oratory?
           A dying art.
Candor?
           Only from mothers
  in crisis.
              Poetry declaimed
  from memory by poets in public?
Miniscule to the point of nil.
Poems performed by actors?
More than informed, the hearer's
  transformed.
                    Advertising pitches?
No less than money talking
  to money.
              Blasphemy?
                          Reserved
  for experts to rebuke the deserving.
Amplified voices?
                     Microphoned
  whispers are whispers no more.
Apologies and thanks?

Heartfelt
at times but more often forced
or routine.
Children's questions?
Instantly immortal regardless
of response.
Pleas for peace
from world rulers?
Words
to buy time for the wars
they're planning.
Eulogies for heads
of state?
God spare us.
Eulogies for those who challenge
the Caesars, Tartuffes and Babbitts
of this world?
Silence.
Sacred,
voluntary, eloquent silence
that is the first word and the last.

There's No Defense

Snow's predicted along with hail
   and high winds.
                     Having sprouted
   barely a glimpse of green,
   daffodil and crocus will survive.
Long past the reveille of bloom,
   tulips will be doomed by dawn
   and droop like the sullen.
                        This
   random hopscotch of misses
   and mishaps revives some history
   I'd just as soon forget.
Linda's drifting SUV
   ran over both her legs
   but fractured neither.
                  Frank's son
   turned right instead of left,
   and it was over.
               At the last
   minute Robert Kennedy
   used a different hotel exit
   where his killer was waiting.
                  His older
   brother spurned a closed
   and armored car in Dallas
   as demeaning to his office
   and chose instead a limousine
   completely open-roofed and risky
   as democracy itself.
              So much

for precedent.
Tulips await
a lethal storm, oblivious.

To Be or Not

An unexpected midnight frost
  plus rain that changed
to straight-down hail did all
the damage.
              Multiple daffodils
  and all the hyacinths succumbed.
The weeping cherry stored
  its blossoms for a warmer April.
Wounded dogwoods and a lone
  magnolia seemed determined
to prevail by holding on
to bloom, regardless.
                Being
steadfast through the worst
of times has always shown me
what it means to be.
             All those
who strive to over-be by climbing
an alp, skydiving from a plane
or proving their manhood
by swimming three miles, biking
a hundred and then running
twenty seriatim misbelieve
that life's the vanity of courage
muscled by nerve.
           I stand
with dogwoods and magnolias
that survive with wounds until
they heal enough to blossom
as they should, but better.

On Dying and the Fear Thereof

I've reached the point where life
   means catching up.
                Suddenly
my grandson shaves and drives,
and both his sisters know what
makeup means.
              My niece
reminds me with a grim smile
that expiration dates exist
for everything.
            The fact
that trillions of lives are now
closed books while trillions
in time will close as well
is hardly news.
             I'd just like
not to be reminded.
                Once
I thought the best defense
against demise was faith,
but all believers and deniers
find that faith is nine-tenths
doubt.
         What's left but hope—
just hope—which says to use
the time we have to do
the work we love to do.
As long as we keep doing it,
   we trounce the fear of dying.
It's like a custom in Pasquale's

family.
They make their own
salami every year.
They choose
and grind the pork before
they spice and season it
and bake it lightly.
Then
they stuff it in casings and let it
hang and cure.
While working,
they talk, joke and sing
in the sheer joy of being
together.
Viva la famiglia!
Viva la vita!
Viva
salami!
Dying can wait.

For Parneshia Jones

PART FOUR

No More than Words Away

Mismatched

As regal as a blue jay looks,
  there's nothing regal in his squawk.
What sounds like a crow's caw
  makes his tricolored blues
  ignorable.
              Compared to all
  the warblers, chirpers, whistlers
  and hooters in the musical sky,
  the jay's a contradiction.
                              Why
  should it matter?
                    The same
  exists at human frequencies.
For years my aunt admired
  the poise of a woman she wanted
  to meet.
              Introduced by chance
  in a theater's powder room,
  she said in parting, "You really
  are a beautiful woman."
                          "Yes,"
  the woman answered, "I know."
Afterward my aunt footnoted,
  "She was great until she opened
  her mouth."
              Next I remember
  a pitcher's opening words
  when he retired, "Baseball's been good
  to I and my family."
                        I heard

a Miss America remark
as she was crowned, "I'm humbled
by this, and I'm so proud
of my humility."
                    In all such flubs
I note a perfect imperfection.
There was the bride who chewed
gum while she pronounced her vows,
the master of ceremonies who called
the main speaker by the wrong name,
the movie star who said his marriage
was consummated on the main altar
of his parish church.
                    All these
remind me of the albatross who rides
the wind as deftly as an eagle.
Circling to land, it spies
a beach and spirals down
with wings outspread and feet
prepared to taxi.
                    Instead,
as if to prove its grace
aloft has no relation to its fate
aground, it manages predictably
to crash, then stand and stagger off
as if nothing actually happened.

Eva Marie Saint

Beside the vamps of old,
  she stands apart—a lady,
  if you will, alert, mature
  and witty.
              Asked how she'd like
to die, she answered, "Quickly,
but not today."
           Noting
her husband's praise for a nun,
she quipped, "Remember, you're
married to a Saint."
             With Brando,
Newman, Peck and Grant
she held her own.
          Later
she did the same with Scott,
Gleason and Hanks.
           Her art
was complementary, not competitive.
Like Grace Kelly, she had
  a thoughtful beauty and has it still.
Acting came as naturally
  to her as marrying and raising
  both her children.
           Chosen
for plays or films, her art
was not to show the art.
The waterfront film without her
  would have been as dull
  as any day on the docks.

                         She
    changed it to a saga of a bum
    redeemed by a girl who loved him.
Kazan directed her to work
    without makeup and coiffures.
Her dress was navy blue,
      a color she's avoided wearing
    since.
            Long afterward, Kazan
    admitted he watched only
    the love scenes, mesmerized by her.
Recalling her performance after
    fifty years prompted one woman,
    whose judgment I respect, to say
    it was "Iconic."
                   To me
    that's higher praise than stardom.

Exeunt

Bing Crosby died while putting
   on a green.
               Tennessee Williams
was said to have choked on a cap
from a bottle of Seconal.
                   Touching
a faultily grounded fan
in Thailand, Thomas Merton
was electrocuted instantly.
Prolongation without cure
   persuaded Sigmund that dialysis
   was expensive, time-consuming,
   vain and rejectable . . .
                   Not
a Shakespearian ending in the lot . . .
Shakespeare himself achieved
   as common a closure by dying
   of fever contracted while drunk.
That's far removed from Caesar,
   Hamlet and Othello who died
   while speaking briefly in pentameters.
In Hamlet's words—and ours
   as well—"the rest is silence."
I had a cousin who saw
   in death an unavoidable, unwelcome
   guest.
          Because that seemed
at best too bland, she deemed
it wiser to confront demise,
like any inconvenience, with a measure

of contempt.
As someone never
self-deceived, she'd acted long
enough to know the Playwright
plots the lives that actors
live and breathe on stage.
All talk of heaven and hereafter
she left to the righteous.
I feel
the same.
Since faith cannot
be faith until it's gifted,
and hope's essentially a wish,
what's left but love?
That's legacy
enough.
I praise the gratefully
lucky who learn how love
that's theirs by choice or chance
redeems them only when it's
shared.
William Shakespeare
breathed from 1564 to 1616.
I've seen his only signature
in Stratford on his parchment letter
to a lord—a pitch for money.
Invaluable because he signed
his name, it's worthless otherwise.
But in sonnets, songs and every word
for every character in each
of thirty-seven plays, he's breathing
still and on and on.

So Many Dances Ago

Thank God for distance, Cheryl.
Closer, you would see a writer
   with a tad less height, less hair,
   less hearing and cataract-corrected sight.
Not quite the awkward sophomore
   you danced with more than half a century
ago.
            But otherwise the same—
just older.
               Who cares how old?
You women know that birthdays
   are a nuisance.
                  People focus
on your age and not the rest of you,
and that's the only thing
they talk about.
                  Your email
after more than sixty summers
was a gift that made a hash
of such inconsequence.
                  It seemed
so wisely young, and that's
the way you were in Indiana.
Today we waken as ourselves
   at eighty-some to watch
   the children of our children growing
   into independence.
                  We hope
and fear for them.
                  That's both

the bonus and the debt that no one's
spared who loves.
                    Meanwhile
the past stays miles away.
The miles stay years away.
Yet letters show we're all
   no more than words away,
   if that.
                While thanking you
for what you wrote from Iowa,
I kept remembering a friend
and poet long since gone
but more alive than ever now.
We corresponded year by year
   from Pennsylvania and from Maine
   but never met.
                    Each time
I said we ought to meet,
he disagreed.
                "Since writing
letters back and forth
has been so good so far,
why not leave everything
the way it is?"
                    Since words say
who and what and where we are,
he may have had a point.

Passersby

I changed trains in Zurich
   where a total stranger helped me
   with my bags.
              "Where you go?"
"Lugano," I answered.
                  "When back?"
   I gave him the date and time.
   "I am here then for you," he said
   and waved.
            Going from French
Switzerland via Zurich to Lugano
means crossing three cultures.
Gallic and German accents
   yield to the ease of northern
   Italian.
         Seated beside me
on the train, a grandmother said,
"Figlia mia abita in una casa
vicino al mare."
             For days
her words lingered like an aria
I still keep hearing and hearing.
On the return stop in Zurich
   the helpful stranger was waiting
   as promised and lugged my bags.
I offered him francs.
             He smiled
and waved them away.
              I tried
to thank him in French, Italian

and English.
                He said something
in Switzerdeutsch, smiled and shook
my hand.
                I think of nothing
now but that and how
a grandmother's words about
her daughter's house beside
the sea stay with me like a song.

The Eye of the Beholder

Saving what was briefly
   beautiful was all that painting
   meant to her: alstroemeria
   in bloom, Michelle and Mary
   in Norfolk, a cottage beshrubbed
   with rye like something reminiscent
   of Cézanne.
                  With seven children
   and her husband a naval captain
   on sea-duty for months, she spent
   what spare moments she had
   at night before an easel.
If all her paintings seemed
   unfinished when completed, time
   was to blame.
                  She had other things
   to do.
          The missing tints
   and shadings could be added
   later.
          Most never were.
Some said she sacrificed her talent
   by marrying, then bearing and rearing
   children—all the clichés.
                        But what
   if love's priorities came first
   for her?
             Did that make all
   her paintings similar to stories
   that end with a hyphen as tales

to be continued?

                Or were they
works in constant progress
made by hand for their own
sake?

       Unfinished but entire,
they owed nothing to the myths
of alcohol, hysteria or madness
as the fountainheads of talent.
Not any were painted for sale.
They simply *were* and seemed
  as consequential as her marrying
  Sigmund and having children
  and grandchildren.

              Anyone who saw
  them owned them totally at sight,
  and the only price exacted
  was the time it took to look.

                   For Jane Bobczynski

Last Words

On the eve of July the first,
    Victoria announced, "We're
    running out of June."
Afterward, she laughed.
The laugh seemed more ironic
    than casual.
                It made me
think that that could be
a final line for each
of us.
                "We're running out
of—."
                Fill in the month
that fits.
                Forget the laugh.

PART FIVE

The Stance

I Pledge Allegiance to Rebellion

I pay attention to revolts.
They clear the air.
                    They show
     that not accepting what is
     unacceptable is always possible.
Even a failed resistance
     seems to me much nobler
     than surrendering.
                    It's not
     a question of defeat or triumph.
Resisters rarely win,
     but, win or lose, they stay
     in mind.
               They last.
                    After
     his stroke my father would not
     accept his condition.
                    Refusal
     let him feel complete and still
     in charge.
               He died, refusing.
Emanuel Goldenberg retained
     the G in his stage name
     so that the world would know
     that Edward G. Robinson
     was proudly and defiantly a Jew.
Informed that his leukemia
     was lethal, Edward Said
     rebelled for eleven years
     by authoring books he never

would have written otherwise . . .
Refusal arms us to contend
    with issues grave or small.
They could be ultimate as death
    or common as weeding a garden,
    shoveling driveway snow
    or shaving.
                    I leave all further
    talk of consequence, rewards
    or deeper meanings to the gods.
I only know that I feel
    most myself when I say no
    to what deserves a no
    exactly when the no is needed.
To those obsessed with outcomes,
    I suggest what matters first
    and always is the choice—the stance.

To Build a Bonfire

The world is a lie.
                        —Various authors

Begin with old newspapers
    crumpled to burn at a touch.
Add timber stacked like logs
    in a fireplace.
                        If timber is scarce,
    discarded wooden furniture
    will do.
                On top of this,
    dump millions of books written
    to deceive, distract, confuse
    or just make money.
                        Shatter
    and shred obstructing signboards
    that screen America from Americans.
Throw in layers of junk mail—
    defunct or violated treaties—
    underserved citations, honors
    and biographies dubbed official.
Include the rubble and waste
    of unprovoked, preventive wars
    that worsened all they were meant
    to prevent.
                Weapons should be
    scrapped as well, thus making
    battles and murders impossible
    except by hand—a number
    smaller than commonly assumed . . .

Now put a match to newspaper
   pages and watch.
                    Invite
observers.
               After the blaze
burns out, keep watching and wait
to hear what the ashes are saying.

Vows at the Last Minute

Because I've become what I chose
   to get used to, I'm changing
   my positions and priorities.
                        No longer
   will I vote for the less distrustful
   of two distrustful candidates.
Distrust has no gradations.
While women are appalled by war,
   deceit and force disguised as strength,
   most men believe that manhood's
   bolstered by guns, cash, status
   and connections.
                 Is gender at fault
   or faulty common sense?
I shun parades, rallies
   and similar ostentations.
                   They are
   to civility what chatter is
   to thoughtful speech.
                 I find
   all institutions—military, religious,
   federal or educational—loyal first
   to themselves.
              Longevity demands it.
Reform comes only from challenge—
   repeated challenge and luck.
Let all prognosticators learn
   that prophecy means seeing not
   the future but the present, and that
   the world's weathers stultify

the best foretellers.
                    I loathe
officials who pronounce but never
explain, which makes discussion
futile.
            I note that animals
kill from need but always
without malice while we degrade
ourselves by doing the opposite.
I claim that politics would be
impossible without hypocrisy.
As for priorities?
                    I engage
with people, pets and plants
to scuttle loneliness and self-pity—
the ultimate malignancies.
                    I hear
poetry in the names of racing
stallions, flowers, Pullman
sleepers, auctioneers in action
and pharmaceuticals.
                    As for precautions,
what's safer than good luck?

At Hand

I've had my fill of Washington
  with all its numbered streets,
  its buildings with numbered floors,
  its listings posted alphabetically
  in artificial spaces known
  as architecture.
                    I'm sick of symmetry
  passed off as order.
                    If history's
  prophetic, cities will disappear
  like Troy or petrify like Petra
  or crumble back to rock like all
  that's left of the Acropolis.
As for discoveries?
                    I'm not expecting
  revelations from the sea or space
  despite the hype and ballyhoo.
Helmeted to breathe, all mariners
  and rocketeers who've walked sea-
  bottoms or the moon survived
  because they took the earth's
  essentials with them when they went.
So what's the point?
                    The earth
  and sky still offer everything
  we need to live as well
  as possible by staying put.
Going elsewhere is more
  a challenge than a need.
                    What's better

than sea-level days where difference
makes a difference and everything
is different?
>   The world comes true
in all its random perpetuity
without dittoes and right angles.
No clouds are waiting to be named
  or squared.
>   Nothing is more
awakening than lightning except
more of the same.
>   No daisy
needs prodding to stare at the sun,
and a day-old faun is innocence
itself afoot.
>   If these
do not suffice, there's still
the spoken world of Robert
Frost's poems and classroom
chats, the notebooks of Mark
Twain, and the perfect elegy
to Felix Randal, a parishioner,
by Father Gerard Manley
Hopkins.
>   That's air enough
for me.
>   It's there and waiting.

Waiting Room

I'm handed a form to complete—
   hereditary ailments, current
   pains, problems with sleep
   or urination, headaches,
   difficulty hearing or breathing.
The questions fill four pages.
Seated by a "wellness" sign,
   a nurse tells me the doctor's
   running late.
                    I pick a chair
   beside a table strewn
   with copies of *Sports Illustrated*,
   Arthritis Today, *Hot Rod*,
   People, back issues of *Time*
   and today's *Wall Street Journal*.
I opt for the boredom of plain
   thought until I'm bored
   enough to read the *Journal*.
The market has plunged, marijuana's
   more common on most campuses
   than cigarettes, China's troublesome,
   the current Bush is a Bush
   too many, and John McCain
   warns that Putin is planning
   to militarize the Arctic rim
   with twenty-seven ice-breakers
   already deployed against
   our two.
                    Imagining a war
   on ice for ice, I search

for distraction.
                              The CEO
of Yahoo is expecting twins,
and slim-stemmed wine glasses
are in vogue—" . . . when the glass
kisses your lips, you hardly
feel it."
                    Compared to what
the world could be, the *Journal's*
world is a basket case.
But then it's all comparative.
Why am I here except
    to learn how far I've veered
    from total wellness?
                              Some
loss is guaranteed.
                         Between
illusions of a perfect world
and human imperfection, I'm left
with what?
                    I sit and wait.

PART SIX

A Majority of One

The Truth of Consequences

Foreseeable or not, it made us
  wince the way that Kennedy's
  public murder made us wince.
We headed for home exactly
  as we did four decades back.
We sat like mutes before
  a screen and watched.
                    And watched.
Overnight, the President renamed
  America the "Homeland."
                      Travail

  and travel by air became
  one and the same.
                  Architects
  competed to design the ultimate
  memorial.
             Pulpit and public
  oratory droned like Muzak
  on demand.
             Attempting to assuage,
  one mayor noted that three
  thousand victims numbered less
  than one month's highway deaths
  across the country . . .
                But nothing
  could blur the filmed moment
  of impact, the slowly buckling
  floors and girders and glass,
  a blizzard of papers swirling
  in smoke, and finally two people

out of thirty-nine who chose
to jump instead of burn—a man
and woman, probably co-workers,
plummeting together hand-
in-hand from the hundredth floor
to ground zero at thirty-two
feet per second per second.

A Newer Order

Biting his cigar, an Air Force
   general was bent on bombing
   Vietnam back to the Stone Age.
A war earlier, he'd firebombed
   Tokyo to ashes, human
   and otherwise.
                  Last week
a Las Vegas billionaire
demanded that Gaza be bombed
back to the Stone Age.
                  Both men
resembled one another: fat
around the belly, frowningly
serious, flanked by sycophants
and affluent.
                  Without four stars
or a fortune fleeced from suckers
at Casino games, they'd be
ignorable.
                  Frankly, they sold
the Stone Age short.
                  Aborigines
learned to work with tools
and fire, hunted animals
instead of one another, housed
their young in the safety of caves
and coped with dangers well
enough to keep the race
from vanishing.
                  Recently we've done

the opposite.
                    Historians confirm
we've killed more people in the last
half-century or so than any
nation now or ever, executed
thousands and stocked the country
with more guns than people.
Currently we tally seventy
   homicides per day compared
   to thirty-five per year in Japan.
To match that kind of savagery
   the Stone Age fails to qualify.
But who am I to talk?
While hundreds suffer and die
   with our assent in Gaza, I watch
   baseball on TV where millionaires
   in uniform play a boy's game
   to keep me shamefully distracted
   from the world we say we're saving.

Wafflers

Directions?
                    One cup of flour,
          two eggs, a half cup of oil
          and a cup of water . . .
                              I choose
          one egg, less oil, more
          water and crushed almonds
          to create my personal waffles.
It seems that something in me
          loves to break the rules.
Asked if I live for the time
          being or the time to come,
          I say today's truer
          than tomorrow.
                    Do I believe
          in miracles?
                    I do but only
          when they happen to others.
As for the masquerades of royalty
          and wealth, I think of phony
          diamonds on display.
                              And what
          of winners and losers from war
          after war?
                    I claim all wars
          create two losers always.
To those averse to differing,
          I say unless we differ
          we become identical as eggs.
Because of that I sometimes

differ even with my differences.
Some say that's waffling.

                        Maybe
it is.

    But that should be
expected from the few who seek
the kingdom come of independent
thought.

           As for the rest,
I leave them to their platitudes.

Day One

It's never easy being lazy
   in America—to learn at last
   that time is not money,
   to see the future as a fake,
   to watch high clouds appear
   and disappear like expectations
   or regrets.
           The culture's against it.
The telephone's against it.
The fact that this will be
   the first, last and only
   summer of this numbered year
   is totally against it.
           America
   means doing something.
           Lately
   I've found that doing nothing's
   harder than doing something.
It also offers time enough
   to let the whole world in:
   riots in Cairo, Arizona
   wildfires, playoffs at Wimbledon,
   birthdays, baseball or how
   a hummingbird can needle
   a lilac while fluttering fiercely
   in place.
         It's all out there

as usual.

           I see it as it is
and always was: absurd,
ironic, vicious, funny,
fickle, tragic and confused.
I leave the meaning of it all
    for after-thinkers to define
    in retrospect.
              They live for that.

In Depth

The sea is stirred by the wind; if it be not
stirred, it is the quietest of all things.
　　　　　　—Solon

Except in storms, it keeps
   to itself—hiding the sunken
   hulks, the skulls of drowned
   sailors as well as schools of mackerel
   veering in formation like wrens
   in flight.
          We enter it
   to row, sail, swim,
   wade, float, race
   or frolic over residue and fish.
Stirred or still, it tempts us
   to ignore its darker reckonings . . .
Years back when I was eight
   I fell from a dock between
   two yachts and sank in the green
   and gauzy water.
          Saved
   by a stevedore, I remember nothing
   but the green surf that tugged me
   down.
         Since then I've thought
   much more of depths than surfaces.
The surface world of faces,
   handshakes, gossip, headlines,
   advertising and the rest means
   less and less.

Destined
to be drowned or briefly spared
we're here to learn what Ahab
and Ophelia learned too late.
Remission happens when we swim
as deep and far as possible
and then return to shore.
To float is not an option.

Otherwise

Shorter than a golf club when I
  planted it three summers back,
  it's sprouted three new branches
  that aim at the sky.
                To keep
the deer from gnawing, I've sleeved
  the trunk with fencing wire.
In thirty years it should be
  wild-cherry high.
              By then
I'll be both boxed and buried,
  and the war that no one wants
  will have been waged, though never
  declared.
          It will have been
preceded by slogans militarily
  concise and easy to repeat
  like "Surging for Iraqi Freedom."
The nouns change.
            The verbs
remain the same.
           Knowing
in advance that war brings death,
  what options have we but thinking
  and living otherwise?
             My tree
inspires me with nothing
  but itself.
         It proves that life's
our last defiance.

Flouting
what it means to kill
or be killed, it keeps on growing
sturdier, leafier, cherrier.

Clearing the Way

I've spurned the usual seductions:
   opting for ghettoes for assisted
   living, choosing a time-sharing
   duplex south of Sarasota,
   jetting to Paris, London,
   Rome or the south of France.
Of course, these have their fans
   among the elderly, but those
   who choose the first, second
   or third seem always disappointed.
It's not surprising.
             After
dependency, division or delusion
prove illusory, they seem no better
than escapes.
           Lately I've thought
of work as an escape.
               It occupies,
that's all.
         And what is occupation
but a way of putting off irrelevance
before the final silence?
                It leaves
no time for wonder, empathy
or leisure.
        Even as I write.
my neighbor's shoveling my driveway
clear of snow.
         He's done
the same all month without

my asking him.
                    He trumps
the vanity of all my alibis
by showing me how something done
for someone else makes work
a gift of unrequested kindness,
and the less said the better.
My thanks embarrass him.

                              For Tom Andres

It Will Come to This

The chairs and tables will be priced
    and tagged, the rugs uptaken,
    and the drapes and curtains downed.
What used to be your home
    will be translated into real estate
    and listed for sale.
                        And quickly.
Before the closing date, you'll fret
    like someone waiting for a verdict.
What once was recognizable
    and personal will turn remote
    and strange as if to punish you
    for selling a site where birth,
    life, death and resurrection
    happened.
                    You'll tell yourself
    you're merely leaving an address,
    and you'll believe that for a time.
Feeling posthumous and lost,
    you'll hope the life you lived
    will follow and find you.
                            Before
    you leave, you'll pace the hallowed
    ground of room after room
    repeatedly, hoping to be
    reassured.
                    And followed.
                        And found.

The Last Unfallen Leaf

No longer green, it's topped
   with tan and tipped with yellow.
In April it was one of millions.
In February snow, it stays
   a majority of one.
                     In a world
   that crowns longevity, it's king.
Younger, I'd be amused.
Older, I'm not sure now
   of being sure of anything.
Who wants to be the last
   surviving member of a family?
Or live marooned with all
   the fruit and coconuts you need
   but not a soul in sight?
Or waken as the mate still left
   to feel the living absence
   of the mate taken?
                    The questions
  hurt.
      It's snowing harder.
I want the leaf to fall.

PART SEVEN

Present but Unseen

Missing the Missing

Old photographs do not console.
They mock.
              They gladden sadly.
They resurrect the dead as well
   as those who look no longer
   as they looked.
              For weeks I've sorted
photographs from decades back:
my aunt, father, brother—
all the Abdous but one—
Albert my colleague—my neighbors
Lynn and John—Harry
the chancellor—and Grace of the ties
and cufflinks.
              Gone, they've taken
back a self they brought
to life in me each time
we met.
              Seeing them now
in black and white and color
makes it seem I've lost them
twice.
              Why am I doing this?
Photo after photo wounds me.
But still I look.
              I miss them.
I miss the people we became
   when we sat down and talked.
I miss that.
              I miss us.

On Second Thought

These are the inward years.
Semestering is over.
                    Over
     as well the military folderol
     of orders and salutes, the titles
     that defined the jobs that came
     with offices and staff, junkets
     to Jamaica, Lebanon and Greece
     or side trips for the hell of it
     to Bethlehem, Granada, Montreal,
     Kilkenny, Paris and Beirut.
Tonight I try to understand
     the memories I made when life
     meant only going somewhere
     or doing something.
                    But why?
Only the goer and the doer
     think that going and having gone
     or doing and having done
     mean anything.
                    No matter
     where I went, my destination
     changed to here the day
     I got there.
                    Countries
     visited, borders crossed
     and strangers met have vanished
     with the years.
                    Philosophers claim
     that who we are evolves

from how we act.
                    I disagree.
Action for me meant doing
   what I had to do—some
   of it important, most of it
   routine or simply unavoidable.
Regardless, why bother matching
   life with mileage, memories
   and recognition?
                    Doings that outlive
   the doers matter more.
                         Lincoln's
   stepmother knew how doing
   should be done by schooling him
   to write and read the writings
   of Bunyan, Aesop and the Bible
   of King James.
                    Had she done nothing,
   Lincoln would have farmed
   and died in Indiana.
                    Instead,
   he practiced law, campaigned
   for votes, became a president
   and kept the states united.
Credit Sarah Johnston for that.
Historians mention her, but briefly.
Few others do.
                    Knowing
   how women shun rewards
   or praise for sacrifices made
   for those they love, I think
   she would have wanted it that way.

French Time

On the no longer ticking
   side of my twin-faced
   wristwatch it's always
   five o'clock in Paris.
The hour-and-minute hands
   are stuck.
         The ticking side
keeps perfect Eastern Standard
Time.
       If asked, I'd like
to say, "It's five o'clock
in Paris."
         I won't, of course.
Wit and the myths of punctuality
   that rule our lives don't mix.
Frankly I feel no wiser
   knowing that months have names
   or that the years and centuries
   are numbered upward or that
   days are subdivided down
   to hours, minutes, seconds.
Five o'clock in Paris resurrects
   an evening that was just beginning
   forty years ago.
        Mary Anne
had ordered steak tartare
to be prepared at table side.
Asked for his recipe, the waiter
   told her, "Watch me."
          Earlier

I'd practiced how to think
in French before speaking.
                              Later
we visited the Bateaux-Mouches,
surveyed Parisian roofs
from Sacré Coeur and booked
a room at Hemingway's hotel
on Rue Jacob.
                    My wristwatch
offers me this memoir every day
at five, five sharp, five always.

The French Are Like That

At times you miss the traveler
  you used to be.
               Those trips
to Paris and Provence are not
so easily erased.
               But airport
screenings, jet fares and hotel
costs have spoiled what was once
routine.
          These days you travel
mostly by car from home
to anywhere and back.
              You write
in the Montmartre of your den.
With groceries in hand you climb
  the Eiffel risers to the world
upstairs.
         Your backyard Riviera
offers a swing for two
and a beach umbrella.
            Otherwise
you're still the same.
          Distrusting
the future as the fraud it is,
you settle for whatever keeps
bilingual memories alive . . .
You detoured on a drive to Nice
  to find the grave of Albert
Camus in Lourmarin . . .
           You viewed

the actual landscapes that Leger,
Cezanne, Van Gogh, Picasso
and Quilici brushed on canvas . . .
You dined with the best of all
French chefs who spoke of meals
as poetry . . .
Whether the subject
was literature, art or food,
you understood why writers, painters
and chefs are more revered
in France—except for Joan of Arc—
than generals, philosophers and saints.

To Dine in Provence

When offered pigeon by Vergé
  himself, who could refuse?
It came stuffed, plump and hot.
I savored pigeon wings while he
  described his daily predawn
  sorties for parsley, sirloin,
  sea bass and quail.
                    "Food must be
  fresh, but sauces give it
  color—outstanding chefs
  must be outstanding *sauciers*
  like Escoffier."
                    In France where chefs
  are food's high priests, Vergé
  was pope.
                    For him, eating
  was just instinct, but dining
  meant pleasing the five senses
  all at once—not just the mouth
  and guts as in the States.
By that standard I assumed
  Vergé would call "fast food"
  an insult to food by acting
  only as a pit stop for the hyper
  unrelaxable.
                    Or, being French,
  would he just liken it
  to sex without love?
                    Since I
  am one who claims that pleasures

are poisoned by haste, I would
agree.
          Why else do the French
dine late except to relish
a meal unrushed and due them
for a day's work?
                    Their restaurateurs
concur.
          Reserve a dinner table
anywhere in France, and it's yours
for the night.
          Perhaps that's why
remembering Vergé's converted
windmill in Mougins relaxes me
the way that hearing Portuguese
relaxes me.
          Whenever I'm alone
with excellence, I never think about
alternatives.
          "We change the menus
every month or two
to keep the diners and the chef
from being bored."
                    Etched
on a glass door behind him were
names of diners who preceded me:
Audrey Hepburn, Yves
Montand, Anthony Quinn,
Kenneth Branagh, Danny Kaye
and Sharon Stone.
                    Asked
if his neighbor Picasso came

to dine, Vergé responded, "Rarely,
but I let him park his car
in the lot."
        Mustachioed and white-
haired, he walked me to my car
and gave me his book of favorite
meals inscribed.
            I thanked him
for the book, the lunch and all
the lore and anecdotes he shared.
Instead of shaking my hand,
  he clasped it with both of his
  as if we were sealing a pact
  between us and said, "With food
  or with words, my friend, why
  are we here except to share?"

                    For Roger Vergé

Lottie

Her given name meant *gentle,*
  but everyone called her Lottie
  except the nuns.
              They thought
  Lottie was short for Charlotte.
As Charlotte she taught, became
  a nurse and spoke with ease
  in three languages.
              As Lottie
  she played the lute and sang
  to her own accompaniment and once
  with a pianist from the New York
  Philharmonic.
              After she chose
  my father, he ordered from Damascus
  a lute specifically sized
  for her.
              I still have it.
She cared enough to adopt
  a Serbian girl until
  her parents could immigrate.
In a one-line letter to my aunt,
  she wrote, "Hi, Sis, how's
  your love life?"
              She died
  when I was six.
              Decades back,
  a woman I'd never met
  stopped me and said, "I'm named
  after your mother."

She smiled
as if she'd kept a vow
she'd made to tell me that.

The Avowal

Viewing our wedding pictures
  after almost sixty years,
  we see some deficits.
                What's lost
  by saying so?
             Though how we were
  is not the way we are,
  we're still the same at heart.
Granted, our dreams have narrowed:
  no more transatlantic flights,
  no climbing stairs by twos,
  no days without assisted
  seeing and hearing, no nights
  of straight-through sleep.
                 We say,
  as did Camus, that life
  means learning to live
  with loss, and that makes sense
  as long as life makes sense.
If not, we're left with nothing
  to expect except what's mostly
  unexpected.
            We cope and wait.
You still find gossip boring.
I'm wary of hierarchies, institutions
  and men whose first name
  is an initial.
          You're most yourself
  with people who are most themselves
  with you.

I think my best
while driving and smoking my pipe.
Today we're near the end
of February, the month that's said
to take the oldest and the youngest.
Robins are flocking early,
and tulips risk an inch
of green.
We feel the change
of seasons now both physically
and metaphysically.
Either way
we trust it finds the two
of us again still one
as always.
No deficits there.

Afterthoughts in Advance

For the house you chose for us
   that still fits.
             For the cycled
flowers you planted to bloom
in different months all summer.
For showing me that feeling
   is always surer than thinking.
For telling me to dot my "i's."
For knowing what to ignore
   and how.
          For smiling truthfully
in photographs.
          For letting
your heart make up your mind.
For not letting your heart
   make up your mind.
          For knowing
the difference.
          For feeling the pain
of total strangers as your own.
For buying a drum for Sam.
For buying the second and third
   and then the piano.
          For saving
whatever becomes in time
more savable because you saved it.
For thinking of the dead as always
   present but unseen.
          For being
dear when near but dearer

when not.
                    For laughing until
you have to sneeze.
                         For knowing
that money is better to give
when alive than leave when dead.
For keeping spare dollars in your
   coat pockets just in case.
For proving that silence is truer
   than talk each time we touch
   or look into each other's eyes
   and hear the silence speak.

The author of books of poetry, fiction, essays, and plays, **Samuel Hazo** is the founder and director of the International Poetry Forum in Pittsburgh, Pennsylvania. He is also McAnulty Distinguished Professor of English Emeritus at Duquesne University, where he taught for forty-three years. From 1950 until 1957 he served in the United States Marine Corps, completing his tour as a captain. He earned his Bachelor of Arts degree magna cum laude from the University of Notre Dame, a Master of Arts degree from Duquesne University, and his doctorate from the University of Pittsburgh. Some of his previous works are *And the Time Is*, *Like a Man Gone Mad*, and *Sexes: The Marriage Dialogues* (poetry), *This Part of the World* (fiction), *Mano a Mano*, *Watching Fire*, *Watching Rain* and *Tell It to the Marines* (drama), *The Stroke of a Pen* (essays) and *The Pittsburgh That Stays Within You* (memoir). His translations include Denis de Rougemont's *The Growl of Deeper Waters*, Nadia Tueni's *Lebanon: Twenty Poems for One Love*, and Adonis's *The Page of Day and Night*. One recent book of poems, *Just Once*, received the Maurice English Poetry Award in 2003. He has been awarded twelve honorary doctorates, and he was honored with the Griffin Award for Creative Writing from the University of Notre Dame, and was chosen to receive his tenth honorary doctorate from the university in 2008. A National Book Award finalist, he was named Pennsylvania's first state poet by Governor Robert Casey in 1993, and he served until 2003.